KU-472-492

This copy of

THE OUTER SPACE JOKE BOOK!

belongs to

_____

THE OUTER SPACE JOKE BOOK!

RED FOX

For Toni

A RED FOX BOOK : 9781862308749

First published in Great Britain by Red Fox
an imprint of Random House Children's Books

PRINTING HISTORY
Red Fox original 2002

Text and Illustrations copyright © John Byrne, 2002

The right of John Byrne to be identified as the author of this work
has been asserted in accordance with the Copyright, Designs
and Patents Act 1988

Condition of Sale
This book is sold subject to the condition that it shall not, by way of trade
or otherwise, be lent, re-sold, hired out or otherwise circulated without
the publisher's prior consent in any form of binding or cover other than that
in which it is published and without a similar condition including
this condition being imposed on the subsequent purchaser.

Papers used by Random House Children's Books are natural,
recyclable products made from wood grown in sustainable forests.
The manufacturing processes conform to the environmental regulations
of the country of origin.

Set in 12/13 Century Schoolbook
Red Fox Books are published by Random House Children's Books,
61-63 Uxbridge Road, London W5 5SA,
a division of The Random House Group Ltd,
in Australia by Random House Australia (Pty) Ltd,
20 Alfred Street, Milsons Point, Sydney, NSW 2061, Australia,
in New Zealand by Random House New Zealand Ltd,
18 Poland Road, Glenfield, Auckland 10, New Zealand,
and in South Africa by Random House (Pty) Ltd,
Endulini, 5A Jubilee Road, Parktown 2193, South Africa

THE RANDOM HOUSE GROUP Limited Reg. No. 954009

A CIP catalogue record for this book is available from the British Library.

Printed in the UK by CPI Bookmarque, Croydon, CR0 4TD

www.kidsatrandomhouse.co.uk

Greetings Earthlings!

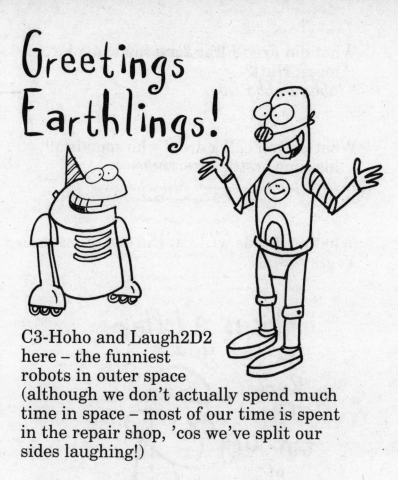

C3-Hoho and Laugh2D2
here – the funniest
robots in outer space
(although we don't actually spend much
time in space – most of our time is spent
in the repair shop, 'cos we've split our
sides laughing!)

We've collected all of the greatest gags
in the galaxy for you . . . unfortunately a
big nasty space villian with a black
helmet and breathing problems stole
them from us, so you'll have to make do
with this lot instead . . . at least until this
book gets a sequel!

May the Farce be with you . . .

What did Fred Flintstone say when he met a Hutt?
"Jabba Dabba Doo."

What do you call a droid who spends all his time on the internet?
E-threepio.

What do droids write at the end of letters?
Yours tin-cerely.

What steps should you take if you are
   attacked by a space monster?
Long ones in the opposite direction.

ARRgh! A
Space Monster!
I'm putting
a lot of
space
between
him and
me!

What's much more dangerous than a light
   sabre?
A heavy sabre.

Why did the space villians go to the pub?
They wanted to play Darths.

What do you say to a space monster who's
   having trouble sleeping?
May the snores be with you.

Who's the clumsiest space hero in the
   galaxy?
Bananaskin Skywalker.

What's Dracula's favourite space movie?
The Vampire Strikes Back.

I'm a space vampire I only travel to full moons!

Who's the laziest heroine in the galaxy?
Princess Layabout.

What do space villians play
   during the summer?
Phantom tennis.

Can robots stand on their heads?
Yes – but they have to take them off first.

"Mummy, mummy – the other robots say
   I'm just a clockwork toy."
*"Nonsense, dear – they're just trying to
   wind you up."*

What do you get if your cross Anakin
   Skywalker with Indiana Jones?
Raiders of The Lost Darth.

Which planet is covered in lots of little
  drawings?
Tattoo-ine.

Which city has the most robots?
Electri-city.

What do you get if you stick a space
  knight in a photocopier?
Obi-Two Kenobi.

Who's the biggest celebrity in outer
    space?
Star2D2.

Which space hero is always sunbathing?
Tan Solo.

What do you get if you cross Darth Vader
    with a toad?
Star Warts.

What do you get if you hang your
    spaceship on a clothesline?
An unidentified drying object.

What do you call an alien with six ears?
*You don't need to call at all – he can hear
  you even if you whisper.*

C3-Hoho: The other robots are saying
I'm mad!
Laugh2D2: Nonsense! You've just got a
screw loose.

Laugh2D2: My batteries are flat. Can
you help me?
C3-Hoho: Yes – but I'm afraid I'm going
to have to charge you.

Laugh2D2: My batteries are still flat.

C3-Hoho: What shape are they supposed to be?

What do you get if you cross James Bond with Star Wars?

Luke Spywalker.

"There's a one-legged robot outside."

"Tell him to hop it."

What do Jedi Werewolves say to one
 another?
"May the furs be with you."

Why does Luke Skywalker's planet have
 two suns?
Just Luke-y, I guess.

Where do space explorers go at 11am?
For their E.T. break.

What's a space villain's favourite game?
Conquers.

What do you call a space explorer with a
   cold?
A hoarse-tronaut.

What do space pilots play when they're
   bored?
Ring-X-wing-a-Roses.

What do you get from the space monsters
  on the Ice planet?
Frostbite.

Knock, knock.
Who's there?
Luke.
Luke who?
*Luke out! There's a bunch of
  stormtroopers chasing you!*

Knock, knock.
Who's there?
Jabba.
Jabba who?
*Jabba screwdriver I can borrow? The
 bell's not working.*

What do you call a space knight in a tent?
Obi-Wan Canopy.

Where do you find the most alien scouts?

Tent-ooine!

When was the first tennis match in space
 played?
A lawn time ago in a galaxy far away.

17

Who was the first robot tennis champion?
Tin Henman.

Why is Wimbledon still better for tennis
than outer space?
It's got a lot more atmosphere.

Why was the space knight fat?
He'd been Force fed.

"Do you think space movies are as
    exciting when you watch them
    on the television?"
"Yes – but it's much
more comfortable
to sit on the sofa."

Why did the robot drink a pint of grease
    before it went to bed?
It wanted to wake up oily in the morning.

Why does a space rocket roar?
You would too, if your bottom was on fire.

What do you get if you cross a space
  knight with a detective?
The Police Force.

I'M a police robot...

Oil-o,
Oil-o,
Oil-o..

C3-Hoho: What do Hutts have that no
  other creature in the universe has?
Laugh2D2: Baby Hutts.

C3-Hoho: What's the space robot motto?
Laugh2D2: "If at first you don't succeed,
  droid, droid again"

What do you get if your cross Miss Piggy
with the leader of Naboo?
Queen Hamidala.

Who's the most famous cowboy in outer
space?
The Clone Ranger.

Which space station cost the most money
to build?
The Debt Star.

What do you get if you drive a space
  monster down the motorway?
Car Wars.

Where do robots go for a swim?
In the Sea-3P0.

LUKE: Doctor, doctor – I was fixing one of
  the robots and I swallowed the spanner.
DOCTOR: Are you choking?
LUKE: No, I'm serious.

Where are the best shops in outer space?
In the Darth Mall.

Which alien has the worst eyesight?
Jar Jar Blinks.

What goes Mooz Mooz?
A spaceship flying backwards.

What do you call a parrot with a light sabre?
Anakin Sky-squawker.

Who's the scariest alien in outer space?
The Naboo-gie man.

when do space creatures get scared?

once in a boo MOON!

Why was the space villian rushed to hospital?
He'd had a Darth Attack.

How do you start a Pod Race?
"One-two-pea . . . go!"

My favourite race is the human race... Delicious!

What do you say to an alien viking?
May the Norse be with you.

What do you call a space monster in a sauna?
Jabba the Hot.

Who's the tubbiest bounty hunter in the
  galaxy?
Boba Fatt.

Knock, knock.
Who's there?
Yoda and Leia.
Yoda and Leia who?
Stop yodelling and open the door!

What do you find on a space librarian's
  desk?
The Returns of the Jedi.

What do space villains inhale when they
   have a blocked nose?
Darth Vapours.

What do you get if you cross a chicken
   with Darth Vader?
Fowl play.

C3-Hoho: What do you call an astronaut
   with a box of sandwiches?
Laugh2D2: A rocket luncher.

C3-Hoho: Why did the alien fill his spaceship with lampshades?

Laugh2D2: He wanted to reach light speed.

Why did the robot put prune juice in his battery pack?

He wanted to keep going all night.

What do you give a lazy droid?
A kick in the Ro-butt.

What do you get if you cross a space villain with a restaurant?
Darth Waiter.

What kind of car does an 800-year-old
space knight drive?
A Toy-Yoda.

Why is a robot designer never lonely?
Because he's always making new friends.

Which droid wrote *Treasure Island*?
Robot Louis Stephenson.

What do you call a person who invites an
    alien to dinner?
The main course.

Why was the baby spaceship crying?
It missed its mothership.

Why is a Spoiled baby like an old robot?

They're both got lots of rattles.

What goes ha-ha-ha . . . bonk?
A robot laughing its head off!

Why did the robot chicken cross the road?
To get to the other droid.

How do you know if an alien has three
eyes?
Ask to see his eye-eye-eye D.

Knock, knock.
Who's there?
Han.
Han who?
Han me the key, I'll open the door myself!

"Have you seen that new science fiction film, *Escape from the Prison Planet*?"
"*No – it hasn't been released yet.*"

what kind of batteries do prison robots use?

dura-cells!

ALIEN: Tell me the truth, doc – will I be able to fly straight after my operation?
DOCTOR: Of course you will.
ALIEN: Great – I could never afford a spaceship before!

What do you get if you cross ten aliens
   with Humpty Dumpty?
Ten green bottoms hanging on a wall.

"Doctor, doctor – I keep thinking I'm the
   handle of a ray gun."
"Get a grip on yourself."

what do you
say to a ray
gun on its
birthday?

many zappy
returns!

C3-Hoho: What comes out of a really
   sleepy alien's gun?
Laugh2D2: A lazy-er beam.

C3-Hoho: What do you get when you cross a robot with a moon rock?
Laugh2D2: An as-droid.

What do you get if you cross a spaceman with a police officer?
Fuzz Lightyear.

what do you get if you cross a bee with a spaceman?

Buzz Lightyear!

Where do they throw criminal aliens?
In the Jar Jar Clink.

Which alien is the best at golf?
Jabba the Putt.

What was Jabba the Putt's best golf
    score?
A black hole in one.

Where do space dogs bury their bones?
In black holes.

What's got four ears, eight legs and two
    bottoms?
A robot with spare parts.

What's got four ears, eight legs, two
   bottoms but only one hand?
A robot with spare parts but no idea where
   the second-hand shop is.

What do you get if you cross an alien with
   a dog?
No more visits from the postman.

what do
you say
to an alien
(dog?

May the
Paws be
with you!

What do alien boy scouts learn to tie?
Jedi Knots.

What did one robot say to the other
   robot?
"I've taken a shine to you."

What did the other robot's boyfriend say
   to the first robot?
*"If you don't get out of here I'll soon
   polish you off."*

What do you call a space monster who
  talks too much?
Blabba the Hutt.

How do Australians travel through outer
  space?
In didgeridoo-F.Os.

what do you call an
alien sitting on a wall?

HUMP-E.T.
DUMP-E.T.!

Humpty Dumpty sat on the wall
And suddenly fell from his place.
He landed on top of an alien blob,
Now he's bouncing around outer space.

Have you heard the one about the alien who polishes robots?
Yes – it's a story of rags to switches.

What's the smelliest planet in space?
Na-pooh.

What should you remember before you step into an alien spacecraft?
Not to get carried away.

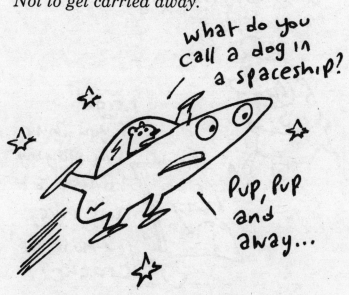

what do you call a dog in a spaceship?

Pup, pup and away...

"Doctor, doctor – I keep thinking I'm one of the cat people from Planet Zzong!"
"How long has this been going on?"
"Since I thought I was one of the kitten people from Planet Zzong."

Why do space explorers go bald?
They don't get much fresh hair.

EARTHLING: Ugh! What a horrible looking
   creature!
ALIEN: I know you are, but I like you
   anyway.

MIRROR, MIRROR on the wall...

Arrgh! If you think I'm staying to look at that mug, you must be cracked!

FIRST ALIEN: I'm bored. Let's race our
   spaceships.
SECOND ALIEN: What's the point? The
   spaceships are bound to beat us.

What do the seven dwarf aliens sing?
"U.F.O., U.F.O., it's off to work we go..."

FIRST ALIEN: Where on Planet Earth did your sister land her spaceship?
SECOND ALIEN: Alaska.
FIRST ALIEN: Don't bother, I'll ask her myself.

EARTHLING: Why are you aliens wearing those red spacesuits?

ALIEN: So we can hide in rhubarb.

EARTHLING: But I've never seen aliens hiding in rhubarb.

ALIEN: See? It works!

C3-Hoho: What do you get if you cross an elephant with a spaceship?

Laugh2D2: Great big holes all over the space station.

C3-Hoho: How do alien farmers catch trespassers?

Laugh2D2: With a tractor beam.

Which space villain paints pictures in his
spare time?
Art Vader.

Which alien likes to breed rabbits?
Jabba the Hutch.

Which space hero has the sharpest teeth?
Piranha-kin Skywalker.

What name did Little Bo Peep use when
she went into space?
Queen Lamb-idala.

Which droid is always buying apples for
the teacher?
C-creepio.

Why was the robot no good at dancing?
He had two left feet.

How does
Harrison FORD
Dance?

Solo,
Solo,
QUICK
QUICK,
Solo!

How do polite robots sit at the dinner
table?
Bolt upright.

Where do aliens get honey?
From Obi-Wan Keno-bees.

Why did the robot pump himself up?
Because his batteries were flat.

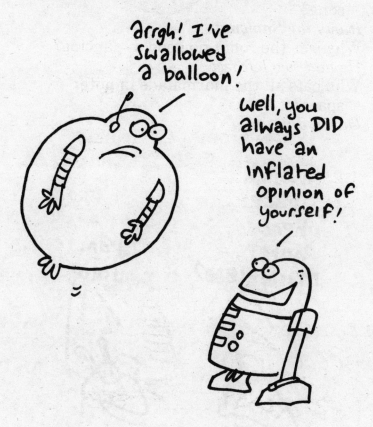

C3-Hoho: Why didn't the alien have a
  pedigree dog?
Laugh2D2: He preferred moon-grels.

What do you call a fairytale about a
  princess and a droid?
Beauty and the Bleep.

What was the robot's favourite Christmas
  song?
Rusty the Snowman.

Who eats all the marmalade in outer
  space?
Queen Jamidala.

which
space
hero
hates
marmalade?

Jam
Solo!

What's got a red face, horns and is only
    two foot high?
Darth Small.

How do you make a robot Christmas
    pudding?
With lots of droid fruit.

What happened to the robot who fooled
    around with a laser sword?
He was cut and droid.

Why did Princess Leia lose her job at the
    bakery?
*Because they kept finding her hair in
    buns.*

What's the droid's motto?
"Look before you bleep."

what's the
spaceship's
motto?

"If at first
you don't succeed,
fly, fly again!"

What do space giants say?
"Fee-fi-U.F.O.-fum!"

What do you get if you cross a robot with
a teddy bear?
Tinny the Pooh.

ALIEN: How much is a return spaceflight?
STARSHIP CAPTAIN: Where to?
ALIEN: Back here, of course.

"Doctor, doctor – I keep thinking I'm an
   alien."
"Nonsense – you just need a holiday."
"You're right – I've heard Mars is nice
   this time of year . . ."

What's big and grey and terrorises the
   galaxy?
The Elephantom Menace.

which Space hero
never stays in
one
place? OBI-GONE
KENOBI!

What do robots sing when they get
   impatient?
"Wire we waiting?"

What do you get if you cross a robot with
   a chicken?
A battery hen.

SPACE EXPLORER:
   I've been flying
   around the galaxy
   for fifty years.
ALIEN: Really? You'd
   think you'd have
   reached where you
   were going by now.

What do you find in an alien fridge?
Jar Jar drinks.

What wears a long black dress and goes
round the galaxy shouting
"Exterminate!"?
Queen Amildalek.

What do you say to a space hero who's
going to hospital?
"May the nurse be with you."

What do you say to a space hero on his
  birthday?
"Force he's a jolly good fellow."

C3-Hoho: Why did the robot stick a
  magnet on its nose?
Laugh2D2: It wanted to make itself
  more attractive.

What is the space pirate's favourite
  saying?
Yoda-ho-ho and a bottle of rum.

What time was it when the space monster
  swallowed the Prime Minister?
Ate P.M.

What's got a long neck, a beak and a laser
  sword?
Obi-swan Kenobi.

What do you call a Gaul in a spacesuit?
An Asterix-naut.

Who's the greatest spy in the galaxy?
U.F.O-07.

Where do space heroes plant potatoes?
In a Force Field.

C3-Hoho: What do you call a dog in a
  spaceship?
Laugh2D2: An astromutt.

who
looks
after
pets in
outer
space?

Luke
Dogwalker!

What's a hungry space hero's favourite
  time of the day?
Launchtime.

What do alien squirrels eat?
Astronuts.

Do space wizards go to Hogwarts? no... Starwarts!

What do you get if you cross Star Wars
with Harry Potter?
A Flying Sorcerer.

"I want to be an astronaut when I grow
up."
"Gosh, you've got high hopes."

Why does E.T. like omelettes?
Because he's an Eggs-tra Terrestrial.

What did the alien say to the large bottle
  of pop?
"Take me to your Litre."

What did the alien say to the petrol
  pump?
*"Don't stick your finger in your ear when
  I'm talking to you."*

How do robots shave?
With a laser blade.

Which robot always takes the long way
    round?
R2Detour.

Do robots have brothers?
No, just transistors.

What did the Moon say
    to the Earth?
*"I'm not going around with you
    any more."*

who'd have
thought the moon
would have a
watch?

a
lunar-tick.

What's shiny and wears a kilt?
Robot the Bruce.

Why do alien barbers reach Earth before
   any of their friends?
Because they know all the short cuts.

who ever heard of a robot with a hat?

well, my hair's getting "tin"...

What do you call twin robots?
R2Ditto.

C3-Hoho: Which TV channel do robots
   watch?
Laugh2D2: Beep.Beep.C.

C3-Hoho: Why did the robot have a lid
   on top of his head?
Laugh2D2: Because he was always
   changing his mind.

What do you call a droid that eats lots of
   chips?
Heavy Metal.

What did the robot have for its tea?
Fish and computer chips.

FIRST SCIENTIST: I thought I told you to
   take that space creature to the
   museum.
SECOND SCIENTIST: I did – but now he
   wants to go to the cinema.

What do you say to a smelly alien on her
   birthday?
"For cheese a jolly good fellow."

What's nasty, breathes heavily and
    charges too much for robot spares?
Parts Vader.

What's the most boring science fiction
    movie?
Snore Wars.

Why did the robot have a light on top of
    his head?
To give him bright ideas.

What is the astronaut's motto?
*"If at first you don't succeed, fly, fly
    again."*

What do you call a group of aliens in their
    underpants?
Star Trek – the knicks generation.

Why didn't the left-handed alien appear
    in the space movie?
He wasn't right for the part.

FIRST ALIEN: On my planet, Pluto, it's far
    too cold to walk and you can't use flying
    saucers because the engines freeze up.
SECOND ALIEN: So how do you travel
    about the place?
FIRST ALIEN: By icicle.

What's the smallest planet in the galaxy?
Tatoo-weeny.

Where do you take
a sick space knight?

To a
force-pital!

Why was the alien crossing his legs?
He was dying to go to the Loo.F.O.

Why didn't the six-armed alien need
   petrol in her spaceship?
Because many hands make flight work.

"Doctor, doctor – I come from a planet
   way, way up in the sky."
*"So why have you come to see an Earth
   doctor like me?"*
"I'm scared of heights."

FIRST ROBOT: Can you tell me if the indicator on my space pod is working?
SECOND ROBOT: Yes, no, yes, no, yes, no, yes, no...

My lightbulb's not working properly...

well, you always were a blinking nuisance!

"Doctor, doctor – I keep thinking I'm an alien!"
"Don't worry – my bill will bring you right down to earth."

C3-Hoho: What kind of stories do insects like to read?
Laugh2D2: Sci-ants Fiction.

C3-Hoho: What spaceships do smelly aliens drive?
Laugh2D2: Phew.F.O.s.

Why would Han never betray Luke?
He wouldn't stoop solo.

Where do the smelliest aliens live?
Somewhere in the garlic-sy.

What's E.T.'s favourite TV show?
Phone Home and Away.

What should you sing to an alien who's
just arrived on this planet?
"Happy Earth-day to You."

Do robots like to eat raisins?
*No, but they're very fond of electric
currants.*

Why did the alien policeman always say
"Hello, Hello, Hello"?
Because he had three heads.

what do you get
if you cross a
spaceknight with
a police
siren?

OBI-BAH-BI-BAH-
BI-BAH WAN
KENOBI!

When are moon monsters most scary?
When there's an eek-clipse.

What do you call a mummy in a rocket?
Tutankha-moon.

How do aliens go fishing?
With a plan-net.

What kind of fish do they try to catch?
Starfish.

who's the ocean's scariest space villain? Carp Vader!

What's the worst kind of bait to use for starfish?
Earth worms.

What happened to the robot with a sore
   throat?
It had to have its tin-sels out.

Why did the alien army send their
   soldiers to Mars?
*So they could spend the whole day
   Martian up and down.*

Who swings through outer space on a
   creeper?
Starzan.

where can you
find the best wine
   in space?

on the
planet
of the Grapes!

What's smelly, has pointed ears and lives
   on the Starship Enterprise?
Mr Sock.

What did Captain Kirk say when he
   wanted a pet dog?
"Beam me up a Scottie!"

What's green and slimy and tells stories
   with happy endings?
A fairy t-alien.

Did you hear about the alien with
   fourteen arms?
She was handy to have around.

How does a robot eat his food?
He bolts it down.

FIRST ALIEN: I hear you visited the Paper
 Planet. What was it like?
SECOND ALIEN: Tear-able.

Why did the alien keep metal polish in
 her rocket?
She wanted to rise and shine.

What did the space monster say when it
 saw a rocket landing?
"Oh good – tinned food!"

What do robot scouts sing?
"Tin can, gooley gooley gooley . . ."

C3-Hoho: Where do space monks live?
Laugh2D2: In a moon-astry.

What do space monsters have on their
toast?
Mars-malade.

What's Darth Maul's favourite soup?

The Phantom menace-trone!

What did the Dalek say to the chicken?
Eggs-terminate!

What game do space monsters play when it rains?
Moon-opoly.

What did the astronaut say to the invisible space monster?
"I haven't seen very much of you lately."

What do you call empty spacesuits?
Astro-noughts.

why do humans wear space helmets?

'cos there's so much space between their ears!

Why don't space scientists like studying
  moonrocks?
Because that's a very hard subject.

Which side of a spaceship is the safest
  to sit in?
The inside.

Which is the moon monster's least
  favourite day?
Sunday.

What did Planet Earth say to Planet
  Saturn?
"You must give me a ring sometime."

Why did the alien put a mouse in his
  space rocket?
*He wanted to make
a little go a
long way.*

What would you call an alien who was
born on Mars, lived on Venus and died
on Saturn?
Dead.

Which space villain has the most
Pokémon cards?
Darth Trader.

C3-Hoho: Which space hero has passed
all his music exams?
Laugh2D2: Piano-kin Skywalker.

C3-Hoho: What did the alien say to
  Robin Hood?
Laugh2D2: May the forest be with you.

What do you call a spaceship with no
  wings?
An EX-wing fighter.

what's red, juicy and spins through space?

a tomato saucer!

Which space knight is always trying to
  borrow money?
Broke-y-Wan Kenobi.

What is Jabba the Hutt's middle name?
The.

Why is the Millennium Falcon so slow?
*Because it takes a millennium to get
anywhere.*

What is a space knight's favourite toy?
A yo-yoda.

Why is Han such a loner?
Because he's always solo.

Where does Jabba eat?
Pizza Hutt.

Where does Darth Maul watch TV?
In his Sith-ing room.

What do you get if you cross a space
    knight with a sausage?
Obi-Wan Baloney.

What do you get if you cross an alien with
    a dog?
Jabba the Mutt.

Which alien lives entirely on bubblegum?
Chewie.

C3-Hoho: What is a bull's favourite movie?
Laugh2D2: Steer Wars.

Knock, knock.
Who's there?
Leia.
Leia who?
Leia hand on me and I'll thump you!

Knock Knock!
who's there?
Droid!
Droid who?

Droid to open the door but it's locked!

Knock, knock.
Who's there?
Yoda.
Yoda who?
Yo-da man!

Knock, knock.
Who's there?
Han.
Han who?
Han me the key, I'll open the door myself!

What's evil and jumps the queue at
  science fiction movies?
The FAN-DOM Menace.

which space
movie is all
in verse?

"attack
of the
Poems"

What happened when Anakin's left
  indicator switched off?
He had to turn to the dark side.

What do space heroes do when they
escape from big hairy monsters?
Thank their wookie stars.

How do space heroes fry chinese food?
In an e-wok.

Why is the Millennium Falcon full of
second-hand clothes?
They are all Han me downs.

What do you get if you cross a space
knight with a nun?
A Force of Habit.

Why do space villains blow up planets?
For ALDERAAN reasons.

Where do aliens find work?
The Jabba Centre.

What did one 800-year-old alien say to the
other 800-year-old alien?
"Yoda one for me!"

What do the Skywalker family do when
they're annoyed with someone?
They give them dirty lukes.

What kind of ticks do you find on the
   moon?
Lunar-ticks.

What kind of bulbs should you plant on
   the sun?
Light bulbs.

When is a window like a star?
When it's a skylight.

What kind of poem can you find in outer
  space?
Uni-verse!

How do space cats drink milk?
From flying saucers.

why did the monster try to eat Tatooine?

Because he heard it was a 'Dessert planet!'

Why couldn't the astronaut land on the
  moon?
It was already full.

What's the best way to talk to a space monster?
Long distance.

What's a Martian's normal eyesight?
20-20-20 vision.

Where does the Martian president live?
In the Greenhouse.

Who starred in the Martian version of King Kong?
The Jolly Green Giant.

what do you call a Twenty foot space knight that eats bananas? Ana-Kong Skywalker!

What's the Martian currency?
Greenbacks.

Why shouldn't you sunbathe on Mars?
You'd sink into the melted chocolate.

What is the name of the UN peace troops
    on Mars?
Green peace.

Why do Martians have two antennas on
    their head?
So they can listen in stereo.

what do
you call a
robot who never
stops watching Tv.?

BBC-3PO!

What's the most popular snack on Mars?
Marsmallows.

Which Bounty Hunter is always making
mistakes?
BooBoo Fett.

C3-Hoho: Why do space monsters never
attack Martians?
Laugh2D2: Because they don't like
eating their greens.

C3-Hoho: What happened to the space
villain who bought a pet tiger?
Laugh2D2: He got Darth Mauled.

What do you get if you cross a space hero
    with a ghost?
Spook Skywalker.

How do space
knights fly to
school?

In exam
wing
fighters!

What do you get if your cross an alien
    with a goat?
Jabba the Butt.

Which space knight is always laughing?
Jokey-Wan Kenobi.

Why did the boy become an astronaut?
Because he was no earthly good.

What do astronauts wear to keep warm?
Apollo-neck sweaters.

Where do astronauts leave their
spaceships?
At parking meteors.

Where do Martians drink beer?
At a mars bar.

How do you get a baby astronaut to sleep?
You rock-et!

which planet
has the most
babies?

ToT-Tooine!

Where does Dr Who buy his cheese?
At a dalek-atessen.

C3-Hoho: Who is tall, dark and a great dancer?
Laugh2D2: Darth Raver.

C3-Hoho: Why did Captain Kirk go into the ladies toilet?
Laugh2D2: To boldly go where no man has been before!

How does Luke Skywalker get from one planet to the other?
Ewoks.

What do you get if you cross a space
　　villain with a musketeer?
Darth'agnan.

What is a pig's favourite movie?
Sty Wars.

what do
you call
a pig
with a
lightsabre?

Luke
Stystalker!

Has *Sty Wars* got good special effects?
Yes – but the acting's a bit hammy.

What did one space sausage say to the
   other space sausage?
"May the forks be with you."

what do you call a pig with a laser sword...

an-oink-in skywalker

Which space hero has a hole in his
   middle?
Han Polo.

What do you get if you cross Little Bo
   Peep with an alien?
Jar Jar Blacksheep.

What do Scottish aliens say to each other?
"May the Forth be with you!"

When do space knights play practical
jokes?
On the Force of April.

Why did the Martian take all his clothes
off?
He wanted to green and bare it.

What do space knights put in vegetable
 stew?
The re-turnips of the Jedi.

Who's the galaxy's craziest alien?
Jabba the Nutt.

Which space knight has a friend called
 BooBoo?
Yogi-Wan Kenobi.

what's an alien's favourite part of the newspaper?

the Star-toons!

Where do space knights store all their junk?
The Attic of the Clones.

In which space movie do classical musicians get hunted down and captured?
The Empire Strikes Bach.

C3-Hoho: What do you call a cat and mouse in outer space?
Laugh2D2: Tom and Jedi.

C3-Hoho: How does Captain Solo wipe his nose?

Laugh2D2: With a Han-kerchief.

what do you call
a robot with a
runny
nose?

R-FLU-D2

Knock, knock.
Who's there?
Leia.
Leia who?
*Leia out the red carpet, can't you see I'm
  a princess?*

"Doctor, doctor – I keep thinking I'm a
    space movie."
"When did this start happening?"
"A long time ago in a galaxy far, far away."

"Doctor, doctor – I keep thinking I'm a
    space movie."
"You told me that before."
"I know – this is the sequel."

That's the end of the book... see you round!

Yeah – may the Jokes be with you!